G000077995

THIS

THE DAVID BECKHAM ACADEMY

ANNUAL
BELONGS TO

....

EGMONT

We bring stories to life

First published in Great Britain 2009 by Egmont UK Limited
239 Kensington High Street, London W8 6SA

Created by SkyJack Publishing Limited

© 2009 Beckham Brand Limited. The David Beckham Academy words and
logo are trademarks of Beckham Brand Limited.
All rights reserved.

adidas, Predator, the 3-Bars and the 3-Stripes are registered
trademarks of the adidas Group, used with permission

Photography by mooneyphoto and Anthony Mandler

ISBN 978 1 4052 4644 6
1 3 5 7 9 10 8 6 4 2
Printed in Italy

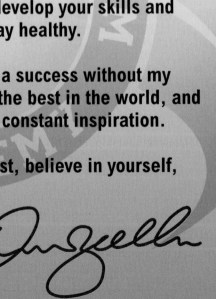

"**W**elcome to the very first annual all about The David Beckham Academy.

Growing up, I was lucky enough to attend a soccer school, which helped me take my first steps on the way to becoming a professional footballer.

From early on in my career, my dream has been to give kids similar opportunities to those I had as a young boy; to provide the best football coaching and inspire youngsters to realise their dreams whether on or off the pitch.

I'm extremely proud that my first two David Beckham Academies are up and running, in London, and in Los Angeles, America.

This annual will give you a taste of what life at The Academy is really like, with tips on how to improve your game and get the best out of yourself – whatever your goal.

There are puzzles and activities to help you develop your skills and encourage you to look after your body and stay healthy.

Of course, my Academies would not be such a success without my fantastic team of coaches; they are some of the best in the world, and I'd like to thank them for their hard work and constant inspiration.

And thanks go to you, too. Always do your best, believe in yourself, and have fun. I hope you enjoy the annual."

CONTENTS

SOCCER STRIP

To look the part and feel comfortable on the pitch, make sure your kit fits! Your boots, shorts, shirt and shin pads should all be the right size.

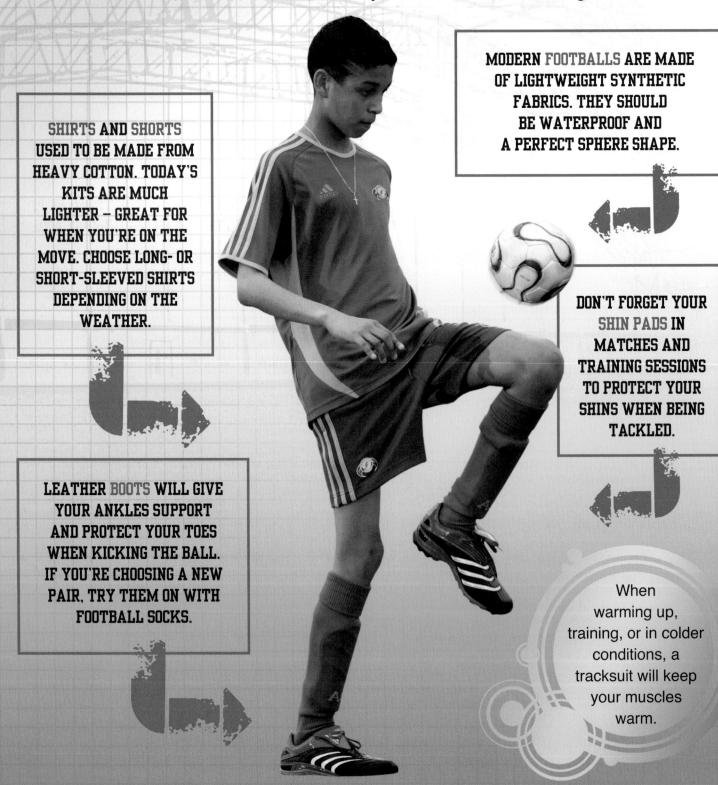

SHIRTS AND SHORTS USED TO BE MADE FROM HEAVY COTTON. TODAY'S KITS ARE MUCH LIGHTER – GREAT FOR WHEN YOU'RE ON THE MOVE. CHOOSE LONG- OR SHORT-SLEEVED SHIRTS DEPENDING ON THE WEATHER.

MODERN FOOTBALLS ARE MADE OF LIGHTWEIGHT SYNTHETIC FABRICS. THEY SHOULD BE WATERPROOF AND A PERFECT SPHERE SHAPE.

DON'T FORGET YOUR SHIN PADS IN MATCHES AND TRAINING SESSIONS TO PROTECT YOUR SHINS WHEN BEING TACKLED.

LEATHER BOOTS WILL GIVE YOUR ANKLES SUPPORT AND PROTECT YOUR TOES WHEN KICKING THE BALL. IF YOU'RE CHOOSING A NEW PAIR, TRY THEM ON WITH FOOTBALL SOCKS.

When warming up, training, or in colder conditions, a tracksuit will keep your muscles warm.

Try your hand at designing a new kit for the players at The David Beckham Academy. Choose colours and patterns – will your kit be plain or striped?

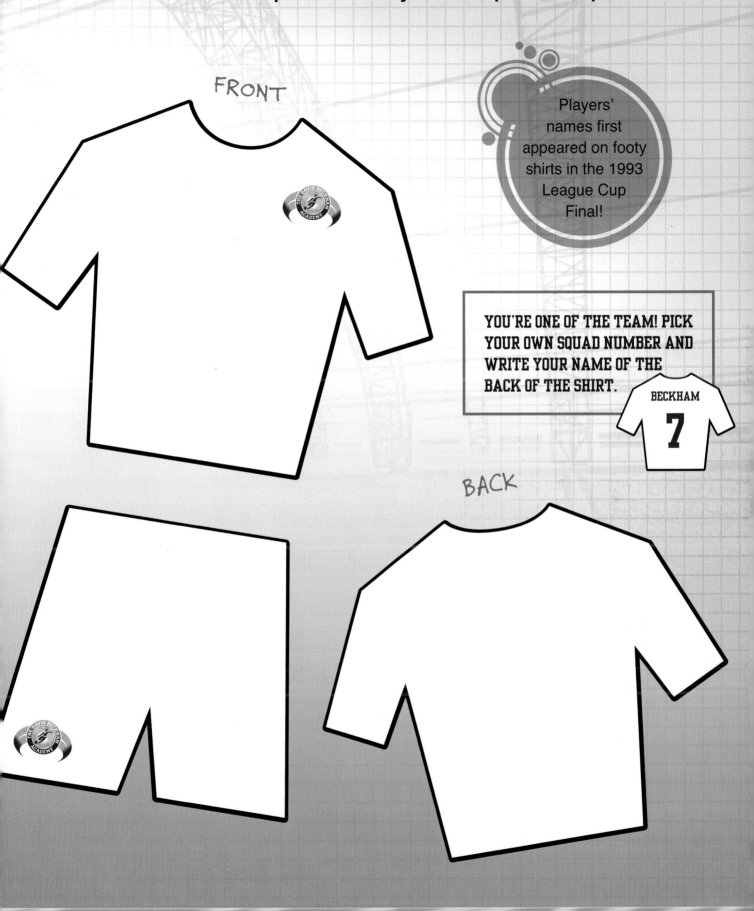

FRONT

Players' names first appeared on footy shirts in the 1993 League Cup Final!

YOU'RE ONE OF THE TEAM! PICK YOUR OWN SQUAD NUMBER AND WRITE YOUR NAME OF THE BACK OF THE SHIRT.

BECKHAM
7

BACK

THE WARM-UP

From a kick-about in the park to a pro game, a good footballer will always take time to warm up properly. It helps prepare your body and mind to work at their best, and reduces the risk of getting an injury.

Start by jogging slowly, then work on your speed with some short sprints.

Warming up together is great for building a good team spirit.

Heel flicks – jog slowly, kicking your heels up towards your bottom.

Next do some stretching exercises to get the blood pumping to your muscles.

Try skipping – swing your arms and take larger strides. This one should soon give you a healthy glow!

Then stretch your calves for five, like this.

Warm up your quads by holding the stretch for five seconds.

High knees – again at a slow jog, bring your knees up to waist height and pump your arms. Try to take little steps.

Finish with some ball work: make short passes to a team-mate to build your concentration.

THE WARM-DOWN

After any match or training session the warm-down is just as important as the warm-up. Players may not enjoy cooling down, but it will help your body recover quicker and stop your muscles getting stiff. You can repeat what you did to warm up and gradually get slower until you reach walking pace.

TOP TIP
Look after your body: always remember to warm down.

TEAM POSITIONS

A manager or coach is allowed to field eleven players in the side, and will pick their best formation to win the match. Each player has an important role in helping the team to put in a winning performance.

GOALKEEPER

Often the first name on the team-sheet, the 'keeper is the last line of defence. Agile and brave, good goalies are strong at throwing, catching and kicking. They may not have much of the play in a match, but must stay alert and be ready to make crucial saves.

ONE TO WATCH
SPAIN'S IKER CASILLAS

ONE TO WATCH
ENGLAND'S ASHLEY COLE

FULL-BACKS

Full-backs play deep in defence and take a wide position on each side of the pitch. They often mark attackers closely and should have strong tackling skills. They need good stamina and speed, to stop pacy wingers getting crosses into the box. Defensive throw-ins are usually taken by the right- or left-back.

CENTRAL DEFENDERS

To be a top central defender, you have to be good at tackling and strong in the air. A defender's main job is to spot where the danger is likely to come from when the opposition is on the attack.

ONE TO WATCH
ENGLAND'S JOHN TERRY

WINGERS

Wingers play out wide near the touchlines. Their job is to run at defenders and use their speed and dribbling skills to beat players, before crossing to the strikers, or taking a shot themselves.

ONE TO WATCH
MAN UTD'S RYAN GIGGS

MIDFIELDERS

Midfielders are the link between the defence and the attack. They are typically good passers, tacklers and are hard-working players. Over 90 minutes, midfield men like David Beckham can cover up to 12km, so they need good stamina and energy.

ONE TO WATCH
BRAZIL'S KAKA & ... BECKHAM!

STRIKERS

A striker's main job is to score goals, which means their finishing skills must be top class. Not all strikers have quick feet, some use their strength to hold the ball up and bring team-mates into play.

ONE TO WATCH
ENGLAND'S WAYNE ROONEY

WHICH FORMATION?

A formation means the way in which a team lines up on the pitch. A manager will choose different formations depending on whether the team needs to play a more attacking or defensive style.

4-4-2 FORMATION

This is a common formation used in British football, with **4** defenders, **4** midfielders and **2** strikers in the team. It gives you strength in midfield, with plenty of width.

4-3-3 FORMATION

The **4-3-3** system (**4** defenders, **3** midfielders and **3** attackers) allows you to have three attackers as well as a strong midfield. This set-up is a more attacking formation.

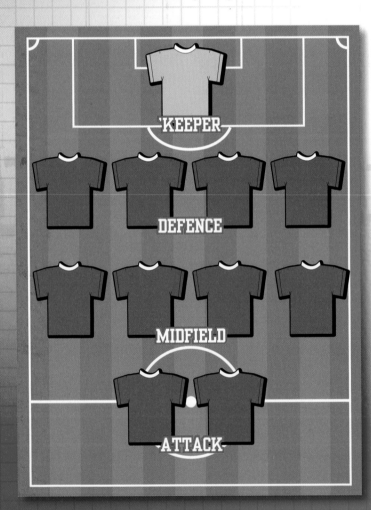

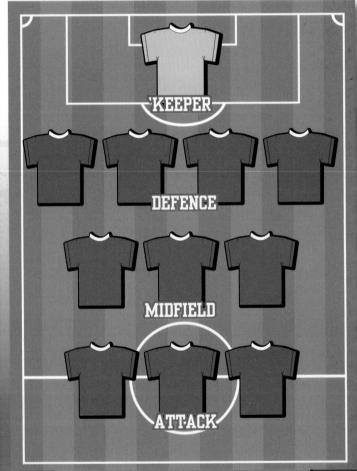

England used this 'wingless wonder' formation when they won the World Cup in 1966!

Answers: A. 4-3-3, B. 4-5-1, C. 4-5-1, D. 4-4-2.

4-5-1 FORMATION

4-5-1 (**4** defenders, **5** midfielders and **1** striker) is often used in European games or for tough away matches. With a packed midfield and a solid defence, opposition teams will find it hard to score. But with just one striker, it will be hard to get goals yourself.

3-5-2 FORMATION

The **3-5-2** (**3** defenders, **5** midfielders and **2** attackers) formation is great if you have two fast wing-backs in your team. They operate as wide players, running up and down the wings to defend, as well as support the attack.

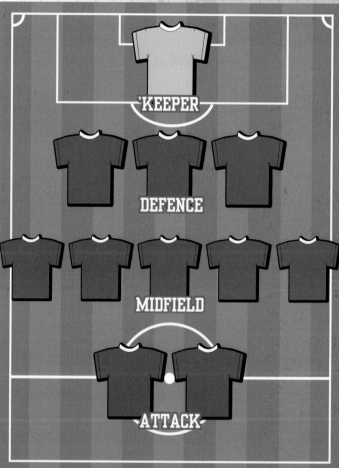

TEST YOUR TACTICS IN THIS QUICK QUIZ!

A Which formation would you choose if you had Torres, Drogba and Rooney in your squad? _____

B Which formation would be best if you didn't want to let in any goals? _____

C Which formation uses a lone striker? _____

D Which formation is often used in British football? _____

USE YOUR FEET

To be at the top of your game, you'll need to get used to playing with all parts of your foot. Choose which part to use depending on your next move.

Instep

The instep, or top of your foot, provides power and control. Watch players like Beckham or Steven Gerrard for examples of perfect precision passing.

Toe

Try to avoid kicking with your toe. This smaller surface area of your foot means your shots or passes will be less accurate.

Classy England midfielder Gareth Barry has a sweet left foot.

One of your feet may be weaker than the other. If you're left-footed (your left foot is stronger) practise with your right foot. Try using your left foot if you are right-footed

Outside of foot

Controlling the ball with the outside of your foot can save you time. Use this part of the foot to take the ball away from your opponent

Inside of foot

When receiving the ball, take a strong touch using the inside of your foot to cushion and control the ball.

Heel

The heel can come in useful when you're in a tight spot. A back-heeled pass to a team-mate behind you can look showy, but make sure you know exactly where they are before you try this move.

BEST BOOTS

**Have you ever wondered what it would be like to design your own boots?
Well now is your chance!**

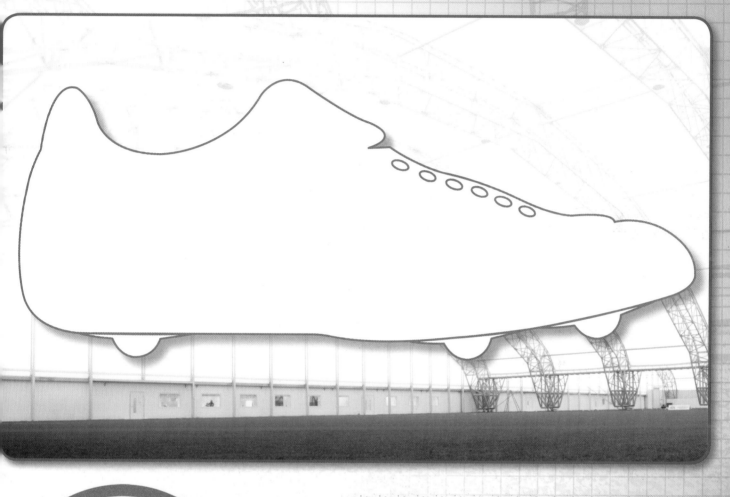

Choose your own colours, patterns, laces and studs to create your ultimate boot above. You could add your own squad number too.

If you master controlling the ball, your whole game will improve. Your touch will get better the more you practise, until you can control difficult passes with just your first touch. Work hard, and stay relaxed and confident.

skills uncovered: BALL CONTROL

1 Practise juggling the ball: start by using either or both feet, and allow yourself one bounce of the ball in between touches.

2 Try to use fewer bounces until you can juggle successfully without any bounces at all.

3 Vary your touch, and try to use the inside and outside of each foot.

4 As you feel more confident, try to cushion the ball using your head, chest and thighs.

5 Remember to stay relaxed, and try not to tense your body.

A good first touch means you can create time to plan your next move. Just watch Beckham in action to get some tips.

Use your head or chest to cushion the ball and bring it under control. Then use your second touch to move the ball away from your body and into space.

If you're tense, it is harder to get your touch under control. Relax and be confident with the ball.

THE DAVID BECKHAM ACADEMY

MY ACADEMY DIARY

Take a look at Jaime's diary, to see exactly what you could expect on a visit to The David Beckham Academy!

2009

AUGUST
Tuesday 18

By Jaime, age 9

9:00 Me and Dad arrived at The Academy. The receptionist gave me an amazing Academy strip, which I get to Keep!

I got changed straight away and went to the classroom where the coaches told us about the skills we'd be learning. Dad went with the other parents to hear about the work of The Academy.

The Academy. Wicked!

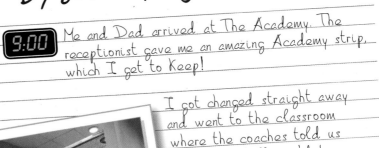

10:00

I couldn't wait to start our first training session. I had butterflies in my tummy, walking down the corridor.

There was a whole wall with shirts from some of Beckham's biggest games, and more signed by mega legends like Ronaldinho, Gerrard and the Man U team!

Champions' kit!

The legends' wall!

Check out these boots – they're the actual pair Beckham wore when he scored that awesome free kick against Colombia in the World Cup finals in France!

The two massive pitches were amazing – I felt like a professional when I stepped on to the turf!

We got our blood pumping with a warm-up, then the coaches taught us some skills – dribbling and turning. It was tricky at first, but the coaches were really good at explaining what to do.

11:00

Time for a snack break! I chose an apple and an energy bar, and washed it down with some water.

11:30

Next we did another quick warm-up and then more exercises, including an ace shooting game.

To the pitches!

Warming up!

Elevenses!

12:30

Lunch in the canteen was tasty! I had chicken and pasta, then fresh fruit salad and yogurt for dessert. I was really thirsty, so I had some water and an energy drink.

Check out the canteen!

Our coach

1:30

In the classroom we did some quizzes and games. I learned loads – what foods you should eat to play at your best and all about how your body works. My favourite bit was learning about tactics and formations.

2:15

Back on the pitch we played a tournament between all the World Cup teams. I was playing for Brazil! Our team played really well together and made it all the way to the final. We just missed out on winning the match, 3-2, but we were happy to finish as runners-up.

Goaaal!

3:15

Phew! We all needed a drink of cool water after that. After a quick warm-down, we collected up all the balls and cones, and sat down for a team talk ...

3:30

We chatted with the coaches about all the skills we'd learned on the day, and talked about how if you work as a team, you've got a better chance of winning.

Then there was a special presentation. All the kids got a certificate and a medal, too, just like this one! They have pride of place in my bedroom now, and I've shown them off to all my mates.

My medal

Some cool pics!

4:00

On the way out we stopped to look at some pictures and letters from other kids about their visit to The Academy. Some of the kids said it was one of the best days they'd ever had! I definitely agree, and can't wait go back again!

Football is a team sport, so passing the ball is top of the list when it comes to important skills to practise.

6 For high (or lofted) passes try to hit under the ball.

5 Listen for a player calling to you for the ball.

1 Hold out your arms for balance and protection.

Look at the target – this is likely to be another player, who is probably moving.

2

skills Uncovered: PASSING

4 Look for clues when the player wants the ball.

3 Try to place the ball rather than just going for power.

When chipping a pass, stab the bottom of the ball with your striking foot. The backspin created will send the ball sailing over defenders' heads.

Hit long passes into space for your team-mates to run on to.

Short one-two passes can be really effective. After making a short pass, move into space to receive a quick pass back to you.

THE DAVID BECKHAM ACADEMY

25

TEAM TESTER

From the 'keeper at the back to the staff on the sidelines, everyone has a part to play in building a winning team.

Find the words to describe these team-members in the wordsearch below.
The words read across, down or backwards.

MIDFIELDER
GOALIE
PHYSIO
SUB
FORWARD
COACH
MANAGER
DEFENDER
SCOUT

L	G	B	N	P	X	B	U	S	J
Q	O	J	U	H	D	T	M	H	N
N	A	Z	Y	Y	Z	M	R	P	F
H	L	L	B	S	R	H	E	R	O
M	I	D	F	I	E	L	D	E	R
T	E	Y	I	O	G	D	N	U	W
U	K	Q	J	B	A	S	E	I	A
O	Z	H	N	F	N	W	F	T	R
C	O	A	C	H	A	Q	E	W	D
S	W	R	T	Y	M	I	D	F	Y

Now look at the letters in the yellow squares. Rearrange them to spell out a secret word, and write it in the space.
Clue: it's another word for skipper.

Answer: The secret word is CAPTAIN.

GO FOR GLORY

Football is a team sport but you shouldn't be afraid to show off your skills and take on players when the chance comes up. Watch pros like Beckham's old team-mates Ryan Giggs and Robinho to see how it's done.

START ⬇

GOAL!

Dribble your way down the pitch as quickly as you can. See whether you can score. Watch out for tricky defenders, like this 😐!

TRAINING TRIAL

Visit The David Beckham Academy and you could train as part of a top international team. But there's been a mix-up with the training bibs! Use a mirror to reveal the name of each team, and write it underneath the bib.

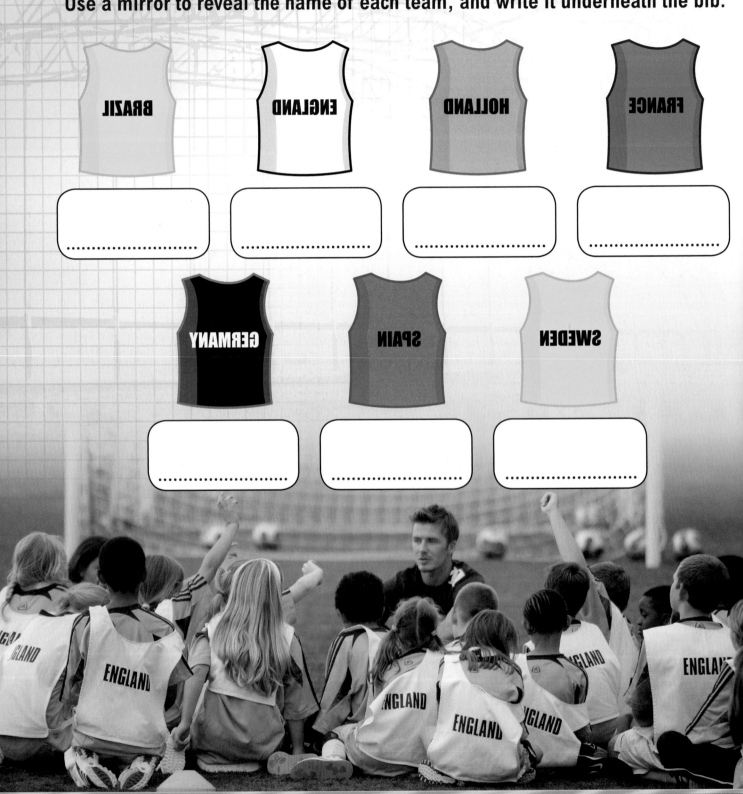

CLOSE SHOT

Beckham is among the best players in the world when it comes to taking free kicks. Take a look at this picture of him training at The Academy. Which of these 4 close-ups can be found in the big picture below?

Answers: Close-ups A, B and D can all be found in the big picture.

Let's begin with a simple skill, basic dribbling. Below are five important points to remember when you're trying to dribble the ball. Remember, practice makes perfect!

skills Uncovered: DRIBBLING

1 Try to keep your head up. This will help you to see any defenders and your own team-mates.

2 Use all parts of your foot to dribble – inside, outside, heel, toe and sole.

5 Take plenty of touches to help you keep better control of the ball.

3 Use your arms for balance to keep defenders at bay and help with your body movement.

4 Keep the ball close to your body, but out in front of your feet – this helps you to make quick changes to direction and speed.

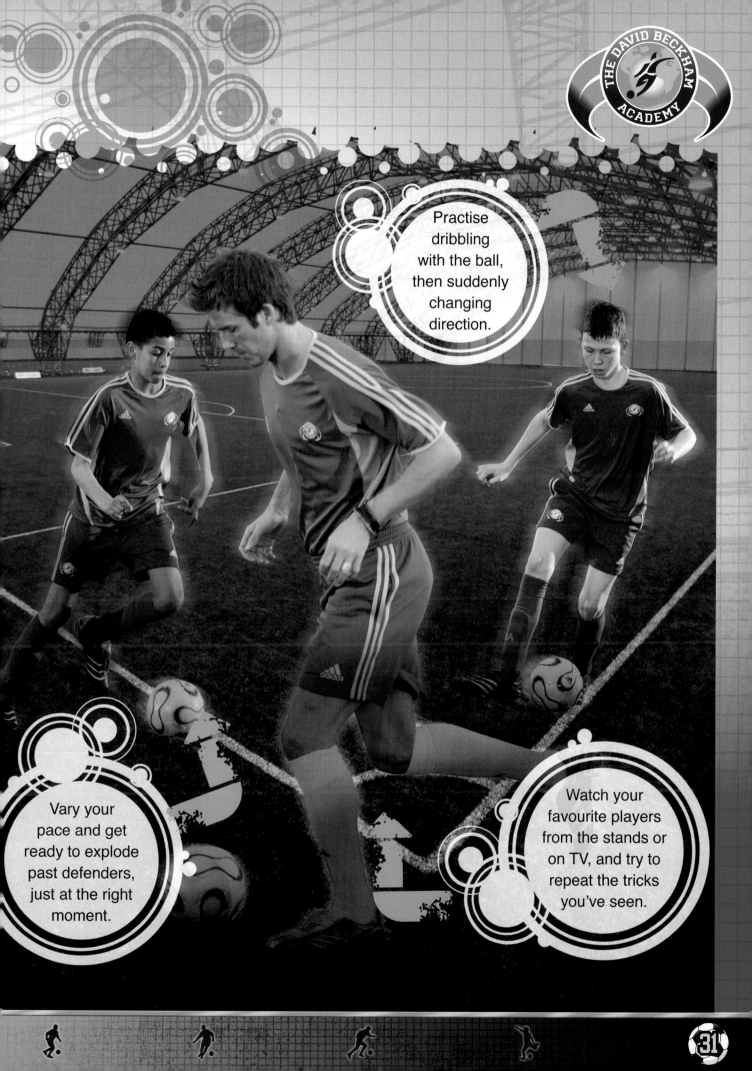

FIVE A SIDE

It's half time and time for a breather. Check out this
quiz to see just how football crazy you are . . .

PLAYER 1

		TRUE	FALSE
A	David Beckham has played for the USA team.	☐	☐
B	Football was invented in Great Britain.	☐	☐
C	David's first pro manager was Sir Alex Ferguson.	☐	☐
D	There are four officials in a pro game of football.	☐	☐
E	Warm-downs take place before each match.	☐	☐

TIME TAKEN:

88:88

Draw in your time above.

FINA

PLAYER 1 ☐

Answers: **Player 1 – A. false, B. true,
C. true, D. true, E. false.**

Play this game with a team-mate or a friend. You will need a stopwatch and a coin. Toss the coin to see who will answer their questions first. Use the stopwatch to time how long it takes your opponent to answer all five questions. If you both get the same number of questions right, the quickest player wins!

PLAYER 2

		TRUE	FALSE
A	Beckham has played on loan for Preston North End.	☐	☐
B	22 players start each pro game.	☐	☐
C	Beckham has twice been runner-up for FIFA World Player of the Year award.	☐	☐
D	A free kick can be given in the penalty area.	☐	☐
E	David Beckham wore the no. 23 shirt at Real Madrid.	☐	☐

CORE

☐ PLAYER 2

Answers: Player 2 – A, true, B, true, C, true, D, true, E, true.

TIME TAKEN:

88:88

Draw in your time above.

EXCLUSIVE

Star coach, Dave 'Shev' Shevel, tells us all about his life on the coaching team at The David Beckham Academy!

How long have you been a coach?

SHEV SAYS: I began my coaching career six years ago. Even as a youngster I used to lend a hand at a football club, helping the football in the community coaches.

Why did you become a football coach?

SHEV SAYS: When my career as a pro player ended at such a young age (20) I needed to earn a living and football is a game that I love to play, watch and now coach. Coaching, especially young players, gives me as much of a buzz as playing once did.

What tips would you give to a young player?

SHEV SAYS: Work hard, believe in yourself and ENJOY whatever you do!

What special skills do you need to do your job?

SHEV SAYS: Flexibility – being able to adapt to coaching players as young as three years-old, right up to adults. Plus I work with players of all football abilities including those with special needs. I also sometimes referee matches, as well as teach in the classrooms here at The Academy. So quite a lot!

What's the best part of your job at The Academy?

SHEV SAYS: The banter between the staff. The variety of the work. Being able to help David achieve one of his dreams.

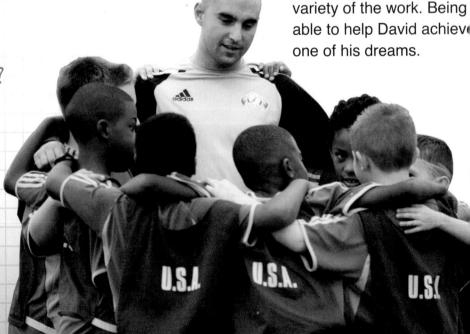

INTERVIEW!

How did you get the job at The Academy?

SHEV SAYS: When I took my coaching course back in 2004, I met Ted, the head coach here. The following year, Ted told me that David Beckham was opening an academy in London and I jumped at the chance to join the coaching team! David was (and still is) one of my heroes.

How long have you been a coach at The Academy?

SHEV SAYS: I started at The Academy in May 2005. It's the best job ever!

Which pro players (current or past) would make your dream team?

SHEV SAYS: That's a tough one. These boys would make my ultimate 1st XI though ...

GK **EDWIN VAN DER SAR**
RB **LIAM ROSENIOR**
CB **RIO FERDINAND**
CB **JAMIE CARRAGHER**
LB **ASHLEY COLE**
RM **DAVID BECKHAM**
CM **STEVEN GERRARD**
CM **ZINÉDINE ZIDANE**
LM **RYAN GIGGS**
CF **RONALDO**
CF **ROONEY**

If you weren't a football coach what other job would you be doing?

SHEV SAYS: Maybe something to do with computers. I enjoyed working on the computers at school and it's always useful to have something to fall back on in case things don't work out.

Which football team(s) do you follow?

SHEV SAYS: I support my friends who still play, so I follow Reading and Charlton. I'm trying to teach my young son to support Manchester United!

Headers are a key skill in the game. From defenders to strikers, all players should be comfortable controlling the ball when it's in the air.

Push off the ground with both feet to get the best spring.

2

Prepare to be brave, and keep your eyes on the ball.

1

3

Bend your knees, arch your back and …

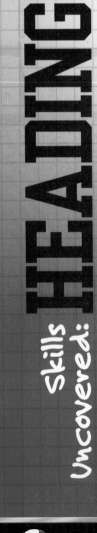

5

Work on your spring so you head the ball at the highest point of your jump.

4

… make contact with your forehead, keeping your neck straight.

The trick to attacking headers is to get down over the ball, heading downwards and past the 'keeper.

Use a softer ball when you practise heading the ball.

Play with a friend or team-mate to see how long you can keep the ball in the air using only your heads.

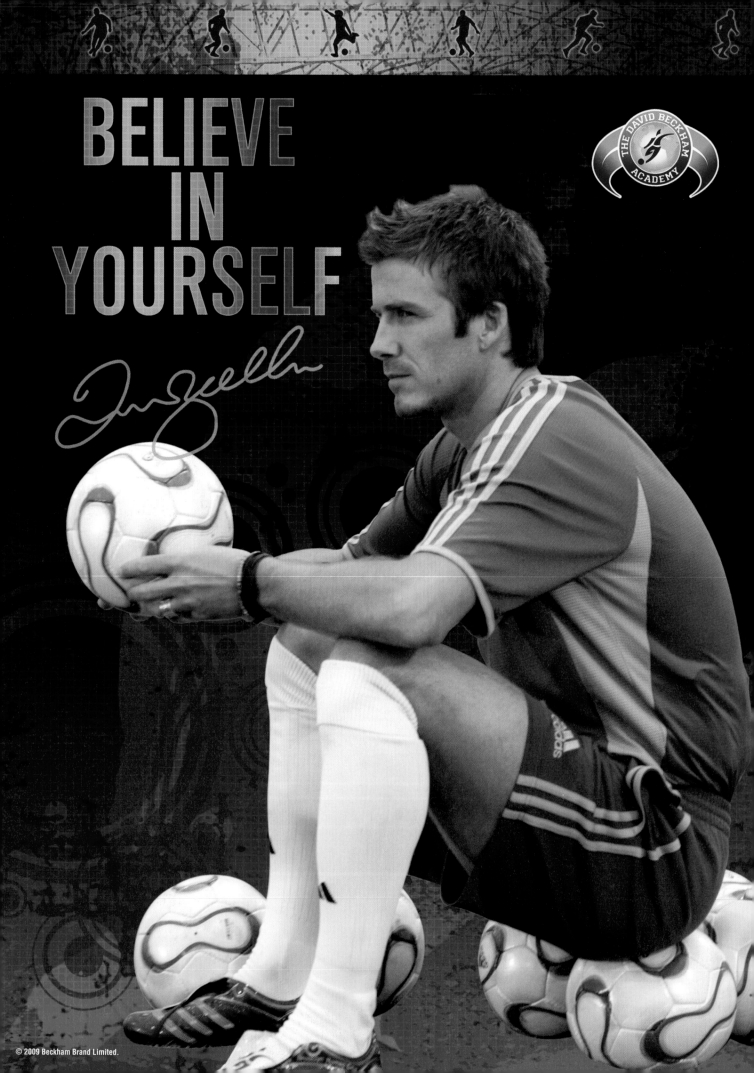

BELIEVE
IN
YOURSELF

© 2009 Beckham Brand Limited.

SPOT THE BALL

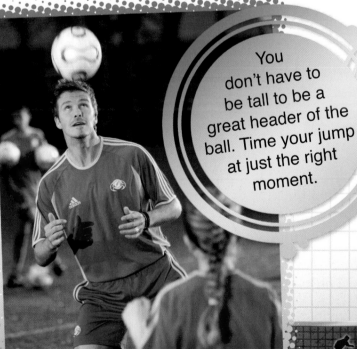

You don't have to be tall to be a great header of the ball. Time your jump at just the right moment.

Heading the ball is an important skill to master, wherever you play on the pitch. But where's the ball in this picture? Pick the square where you think it should be.

Answer: 1C.

39

Tackling is not just down to defenders, some great defensive work can be done by midfielders and strikers too. If your team loses possession, every player must work hard to win back the ball – which means knowing how to make a clean tackle!

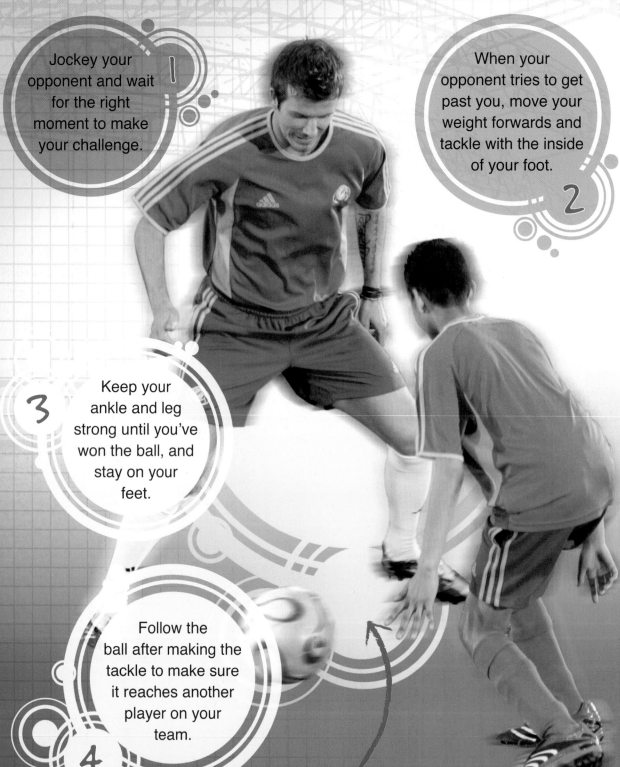

1. Jockey your opponent and wait for the right moment to make your challenge.

2. When your opponent tries to get past you, move your weight forwards and tackle with the inside of your foot.

3. Keep your ankle and leg strong until you've won the ball, and stay on your feet.

4. Follow the ball after making the tackle to make sure it reaches another player on your team.

BLOCK TACKLES

TACKLING

skills Uncovered:

This tackle is all about timing, so make sure you time your challenge exactly right – don't just dive in.

1

Come from the side, across the path of the defender. Tackle from behind and you're likely to be shown a red card.

2

Use the leg farthest away from your opponent to hook the ball away as you slide in.

3

Get back on your feet and into position as quickly as you can.

4

SLIDING TACKLES

THE DAVID BECKHAM ACADEMY

FITNESS FOOD

Keeping fit is not just about how much time you spend playing sport – if you don't eat well, your body won't work at its best.

1

Check out The Academy canteen … where the food is healthy and tasty too. Look closely. Can you spot 6 differences in picture 2?

2

BECKHAM'S FAVOURITE MEALS

Pasta with tomato and vegetable sauce

Roast chicken dinner

Answers: The boy's top has changed colour and the writing and the stripe is missing from the other boy's top, writing is missing from the girl's bib, a boy in the background has disappeared, the things on the board have gone.

HIGH FIVE!

Try to get at least five servings of fruit and vegetables into your daily diet – three portions of veg and two of fruit. Choose different colours and taste new foods too.

1 PORTION OF FRUIT
1 PORTION OF VEG

Fill in the chart every day for a week to see your 5-a-day food score. Cross out a box for every fruit or vegetable you eat.

TOP TIPS

Mix it up – try fresh fruit smoothies!
Dried fruit like raisins or apricots make great snacks. Juice boxes with 100% pure fruit juice should quench your thirst.

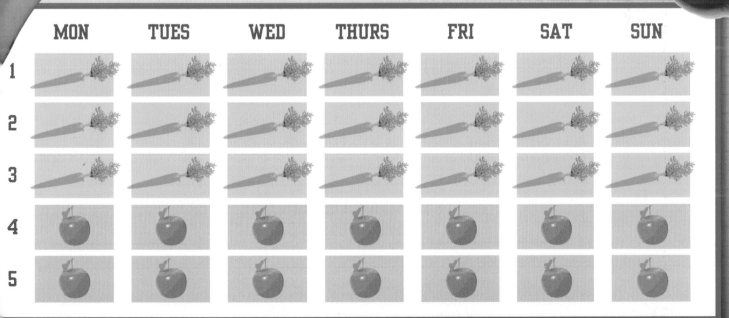

	MON	TUES	WED	THURS	FRI	SAT	SUN
1							
2							
3							
4							
5							

REMEMBER, 1 HANDFUL = 1 PORTION!

FOOTY FUEL

Nurition is really important for any footballer. Each pro team has a nutritionist, whose job it is to make sure the players are getting the foods and drink they need to help them perform at their best.

Take a look at this food list. Which is the superstar food each time?
Tick ☑ ones you think are right and leave the others on the subs bench.

☐	MASHED POTATO	V	CHIPS	☐
☐	CEREAL BAR	V	CHOCOLATE BAR	☐
☐	GRILLED CHICKEN	V	FRIED CHICKEN	☐
☐	FRESH FRUIT SALAD	V	ICE CREAM	☐
☐	FRIED EGG	V	BOILED EGG	☐
☐	THIN CRUST VEGGIE PIZZA	V	STUFFED CRUST CHEESE PIZZA	☐
☐	CRISPS	V	DRIED FRUIT & NUTS	☐
☐	FIZZY DRINK	V	SMOOTHIE	☐

TOP TIP
Always eat breakfast to give your body the fuel it needs and never skimp on taking on fluids.

Answers: Mashed potato, cereal bar, grilled chicken, fresh fruit salad, boiled egg, thin crust veggie pizza, dried fruit and nuts, smoothie.

KEEP ON GOING

© 2009 Beckham Brand Limited.

A quick turn with the ball can create space in a flash and leave the defence flat-footed. It's a great skill to practise to trick defenders, even if you have your back to goal.

TURNING

skills Uncovered:

1 Running at pace, use your first touch to take the ball to the side.

2 Next put the foot furthest away from your opponent on top of the ball to stop it.

5 Take the ball into space using your other foot to push the ball out in front of you.

4 Use your planted foot to pivot and push off with, turning your body.

3 Drag the ball back through your legs so you're facing the way you came.

STOP TURNS

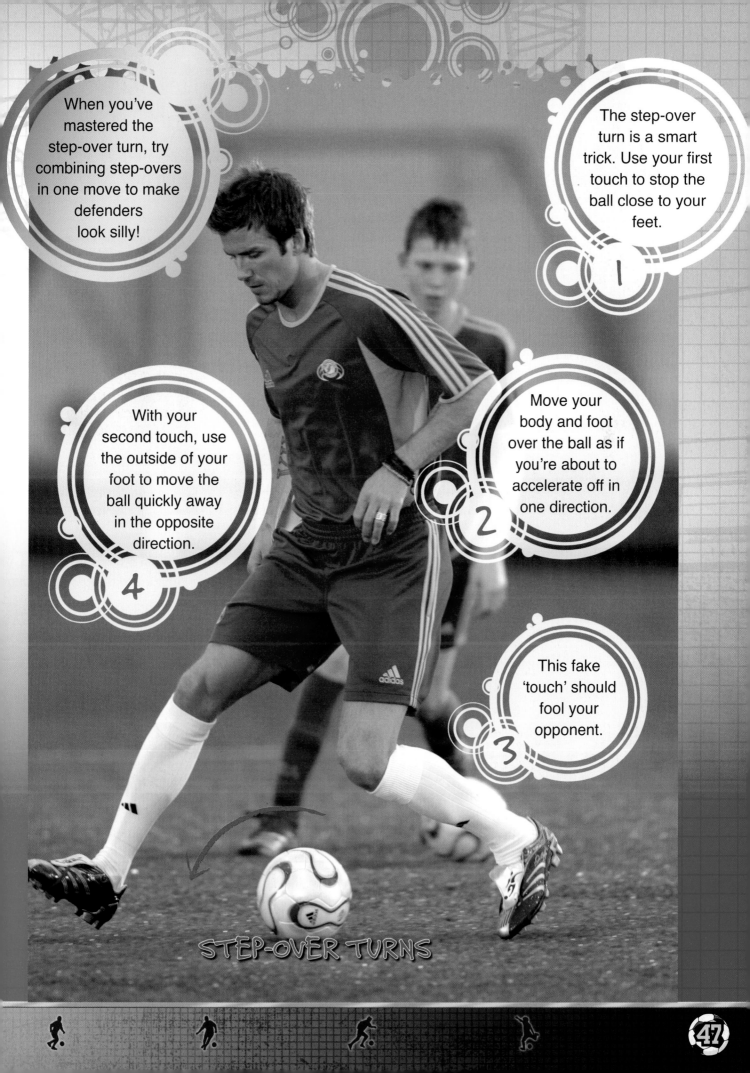

When you've mastered the step-over turn, try combining step-overs in one move to make defenders look silly!

The step-over turn is a smart trick. Use your first touch to stop the ball close to your feet.

1

With your second touch, use the outside of your foot to move the ball quickly away in the opposite direction.

4

Move your body and foot over the ball as if you're about to accelerate off in one direction.

2

This fake 'touch' should fool your opponent.

3

STEP-OVER TURNS

TWIN TROUBLE!

Identical twins Adam and James Parker are on the most exciting journey of their lives. The day has finally arrived – the football-mad brothers are on their way to The David Beckham Academy.

JAMES, A TALENTED PLAYER, IS SHOWING OFF. AS USUAL …

I CAN'T WAIT TO GET ON THE PITCH. JUST DON'T SHOW ME UP WITH YOUR TWO LEFT FEET, OK, ADAM?

I COULDN'T HELP SCORING THAT OWN GOAL THE LAST TIME WE PLAYED!

SO I'M NOT AS GOOD AS JAMES, SO WHAT? I'M GOING TO HAVE FUN PLAYING TODAY, ADAM THINKS.

AS THEY ROUND ONE LAST CORNER, THE ENORMOUS ARCHES OF THE ACADEMY COME INTO VIEW …

AWESOME!

INSIDE THE ACADEMY, SHIRTS SIGNED BY THE GAME'S TOP PROS HANG ON THE WALL …

"CHECK THIS ONE OUT, BECKHAM WORE THIS ACTUAL SHIRT!" SAYS JAMES.
"COOL! I WONDER IF HE'S HERE," ADAM GRINS.
"YEAH RIGHT. AS IF!" LAUGHS JAMES.

JUST THEN …

I'M FRANK, HEAD COACH HERE.

FRANK TELLS THEM ABOUT THE AFTERNOON TOURNAMENT. THERE'S A TROPHY FOR THE WINNING TEAM UP FOR GRABS …

AND THE TOP SCORER WILL WIN THE 'GOLDEN BOOT'

JAMES AND ADAM ARE PICKED FOR THE SAME TEAM, 'SPAIN'.

HEY, WHERE DID YOU GET THOSE BOOTS?

LATER IN THE CHANGING ROOMS, ADAM LACES UP A PAIR OF BRAND-NEW PREDATOR BOOTS …

OFF DAD. THEY'RE AN 'INVESTMENT'!

BACK ON THE PITCH, THE COACH CALLS ADAM TO ONE SIDE ...

YOU'RE A GREAT TEAM PLAYER. BELIEVE IN YOURSELF.

"ANY FREE KICK YOU TAKE WITH THAT RIGHT FOOT WILL BE UNSTOPPABLE," HE SAYS.

ADAM NODS. *SOMEONE BELIEVES IN ME!*

OK, COACH!

TIME FOR THE FINAL, AND IT'S HOLLAND V SPAIN.

THE GAME BEGINS AT A FRANTIC PACE AND BOTH TEAMS SCORE AN EARLY GOAL. BY THE 85TH MINUTE THE SCORES ARE STILL TIED, UNTIL STUDSY SHRUGS ADAM OFF THE BALL AND GETS HIS SECOND GOAL OF THE MATCH TO PUT HOLLAND 2–1 UP.

ADAM IS DETERMINED NOT TO GIVE UP. HE REMEMBERS THE COACH'S WORDS: *BELIEVE IN YOURSELF.*

AS STUDSY STEAMS TOWARDS HIM, ADAM TIMES HIS TACKLE PERFECTLY, AND WINS THE BALL. THEN WITH A QUICK FLICK, HE PASSES TO JAMES, WHO GOES FOR A SPECTACULAR OVERHEAD KICK ...

THE NET BULGES AND THE CROWD ROARS. GOAL! THE TEAMS ARE BACK ON LEVEL TERMS, 2–2!

KICK!

UH-OH!

TAKE THAT!

AS THE GAME KICKS OFF AGAIN, STUDSY PUTS IN A CRUNCHING TACKLE, BRINGING HIS BOOT DOWN HARD ON JAMES' ANKLE.

IT SPELLS THE END OF THE MATCH FOR JAMES ... AND STUDSY.

"YOU'RE OFF!" SAYS THE REF, FLASHING STUDSY A RED CARD.

ADAM HELPS JAMES LIMP OFF THE PITCH. WITH THEIR STAR PLAYER OUT OF ACTION, WHO COULD POSSIBLY FILL HIS BOOTS?

CRUNCH!

50

M THINKS ON HIS FEET ...

QUICK, GIVE ME YOUR BOOTS. THERE'S NO TIME TO EXPLAIN ...

HE PUTS ON JAMES' BOOTS AND JOGS BACK ON THE PITCH, PRETENDING TO LIMP SLIGHTLY.

"GOOD LUCK!" CALLS JAMES.

ADAM SMILES BACK. *HE'S STILL MY BROTHER,* HE THINKS.

PLACING THE BALL NERVOUSLY ON THE GROUND, ADAM TRIES TO STEADY HIS NERVES. *I'VE GOT TO DO THIS. FOR JAMES, FOR THE TEAM AND FOR MYSELF.*

YOU CAN DO IT, JAMES!

ADAM EYES UP THE NET. *IF I CAN CURVE THE BALL INTO THAT TINY GAP IN THE TOP LEFT-HAND CORNER, SPAIN WILL WIN THE TOURNAMENT AND THE GOLDEN BOOT TROPHY WILL BELONG TO JAMES,* HE SAYS TO HIMSELF.

TAKING A DEEP BREATH, ADAM STARTS HIS RUN-UP ...

HIS FOOT STRIKES THE BALL AND THE SHOT SAILS TOWARDS THE GOAL, AS IF IN SLOW MOTION ...

THE 'KEEPER DIVES THROUGH THE AIR AT FULL STRETCH ...

"GOAL!" ADAM HEARS, AND TEAM SPAIN RUN UP TO CONGRATULATE HIM.

SECONDS LATER, THE FINAL WHISTLE GOES.

"YOU DID IT, JAMES!" THEY CHEER. "YOU WON THE GOLDEN BOOT!"

NO ONE REALISES THAT ADAM TOOK THE FREE KICK! ONLY THE TWINS KNOW THE TRUTH ...

T'S IN!

CONGRATULATIONS, BOYS!

WOW, THANK YOU!

AMID THE CELEBRATIONS, THE COACH ANNOUNCES A SURPRISE ... "HERE TO PRESENT THE TROPHIES TODAY, MR DAVID BECKHAM!"

JAMES SWALLOWS HARD. *IT WASN'T ME WHO SCORED THAT FINAL GOAL, I'VE GOT TO OWN UP,* HE THINKS.

THE TWINS TELL THE COACH THE TRUTH ... "YOU'D BETTER BOTH GO COLLECT THE TROPHY THEN," HE SAYS, AFTER MAKING THEM SWEAT FOR A MINUTE.

"LOOKS LIKE YOU BOTH DESERVE THIS," SMILES DAVID. "I COULDN'T HAVE SCORED A BETTER FREE KICK MYSELF."

THE TWINS HOLD THE TROPHY ABOVE THEIR HEADS.

"WE MAKE A PRETTY GOOD TEAM, DON'T YOU THINK?" SAYS JAMES.

"UNBEATABLE!" SMILES ADAM.

YOUR BODY

The team physiotherapist, or physio for short, has a very important job. They need to know all about the human body to help players stay healthy and avoid injuries. They need more than just a magic sponge!

Which one of these jobs does a physio not do?
Put a cross in the box next to the wrong job ☒.

- [ ] STUDIES BONES AND MUSCLES
- [ ] TREATS INJURED PLAYERS
- [ ] DRIVES THE TEAM BUS
- [ ] HELPS PLAYERS PREVENT INJURIES
- [ ] MEASURES PLAYERS' HEART RATES

· PHYSIO ROOM ·

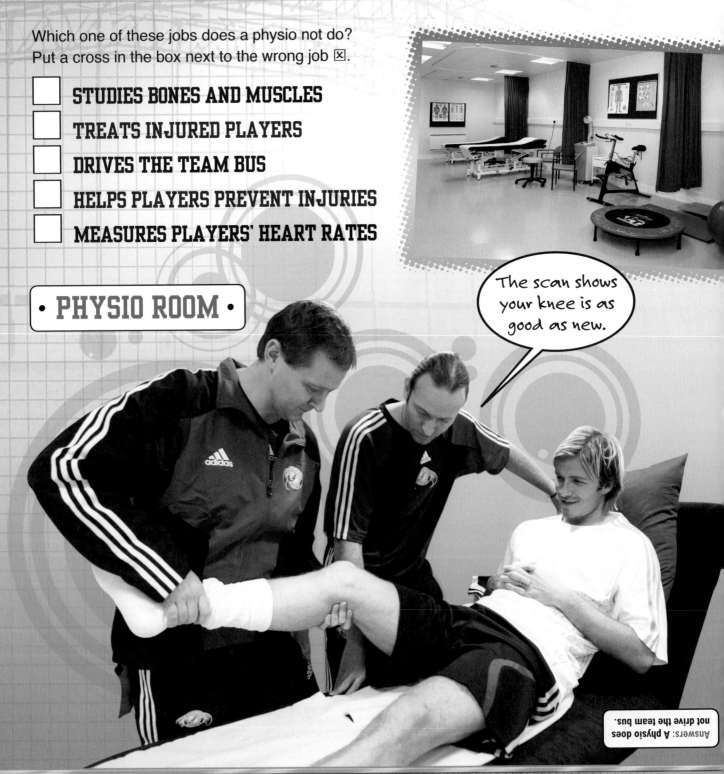

The scan shows your knee is as good as new.

Answers: A physio does not drive the team bus.

Visit The Academy and you'll learn all about the human body – bones, muscles and more! Look closely, one of these pictures is different from the rest. Can you spot the odd one out?

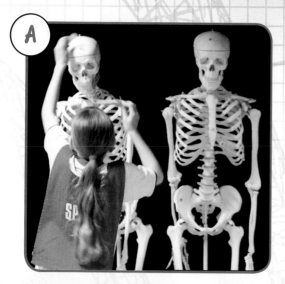

A

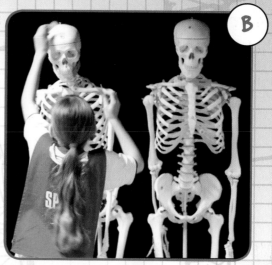

B

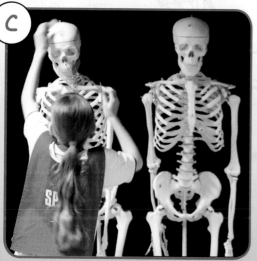

C

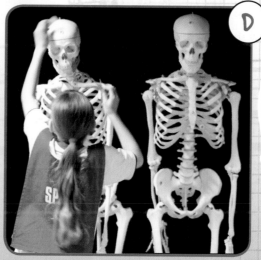

D

DID YOU KNOW?
A human skeleton has over 200 bones!

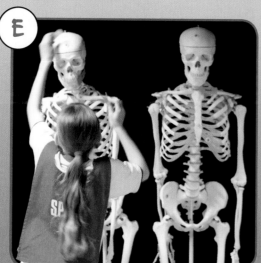

E

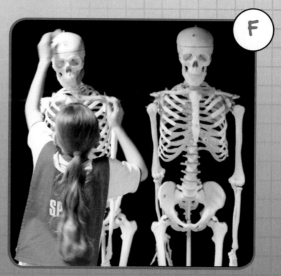

F

Volleying is a difficult skill to perfect, as striking a ball that's still in the air needs good technique. Time it right, though, and you can catch the best of 'keepers off guard.

5 Strike the ball at the centre or towards the top, keeping your head over the ball.

6 Follow through in the direction of the goal.

1 Keep your eyes on the flight of the ball while you get into position.

4 Lead with your knee and bring the kicking leg through.

VOLLEYING

skills Uncovered:

3 Keep your non-striking foot planted firmly on the ground.

2 Use your arms for balance and imagine a point in front of you where you're going to strike the ball.

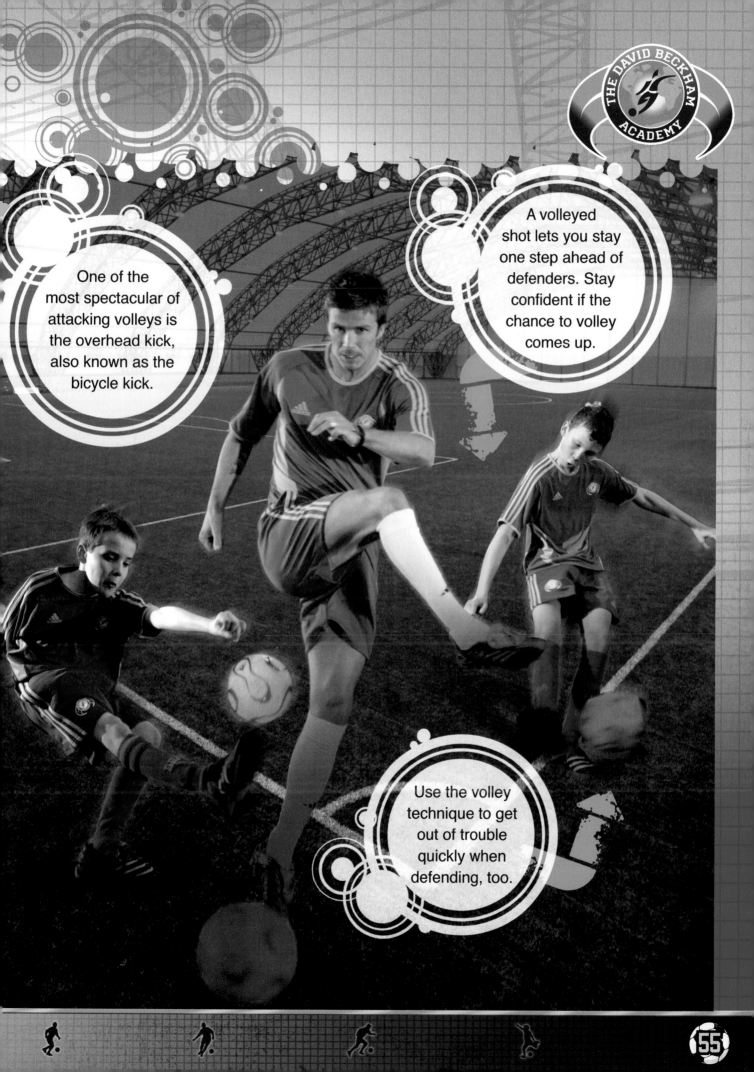

One of the most spectacular of attacking volleys is the overhead kick, also known as the bicycle kick.

A volleyed shot lets you stay one step ahead of defenders. Stay confident if the chance to volley comes up.

Use the volley technique to get out of trouble quickly when defending, too.

BRAIN BUSTER!

How many times can you find the word BALL in this brain-busting puzzle? It can read forwards, backwards, up, down and diagonally.

Answer: ball appears 14 times.

Write your answer here:

SHADOW PLAY

**The only way to improve your skills is to practise.
Keep on going until you master the move.**

Take a look at these training moves. Can you match each move
to its shadow? Look back through the Annual to help you.

WARMING UP

DRIBBLING

JUGGLING THE BALL

TURNING

SHOOTING

PASSING

Answers: A – Dribbling, B – Passing, C – Turning, D – Shooting, E – Warming Up, F – Juggling the ball.

The aim of the game in football? To score goals! When you find yourself in a goal-scoring situation, remember these top tips …

5 Follow through with both the striking foot and the body.

1 Go for accuracy rather than power, and aim your shots low and to the corners of the goal.

4 Keep your head down and eyes on the ball at the moment of impact.

Look to see if the 'keeper has left a gap on either side of the goal.

2

STRIKING

skills Uncovered:

3 Approach the ball at a slight angle and strike with the instep (laces) of your boots.

Don't worry if your shot hits the post or bar, your team-mates should be in position to snap up the rebound.

To be a sharp-shooter you'll need to be confident, so believe you'll hit the back of the net with every strike.

The more shots you take, the more likely you are to score a goal. Simple!

THE DAVID BECKHAM ACADEMY

QUICK DRAW

Time to grab your pens and show some creative flair! Using the grid to help you, copy the smart David Beckham Academy logo into the box below.

DID YOU KNOW?

On an international shirt, the number of stars tells you how many times the team's won the World Cup!

FLY THE FLAG

Over his professional career, David Beckham has played in the top league in four different countries. Unscramble the words to find the name of each country, then write the name of the club below.

YALIT

COUNTRY:
_____

CLUB:
_____

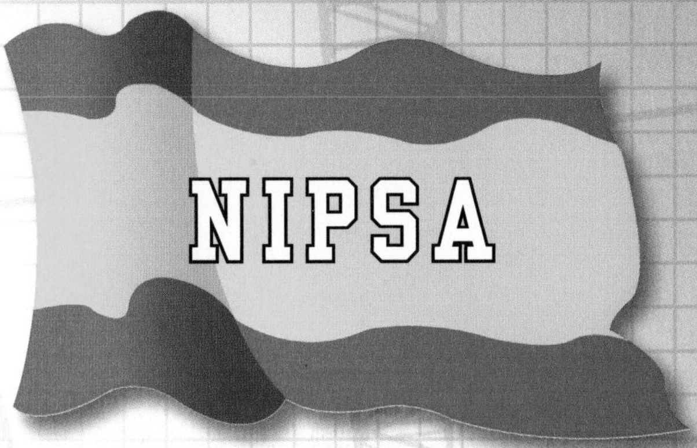

NIPSA

COUNTRY:
_____

CLUB:
_____

DANLEGN

COUNTRY:
_____

CLUB:
_____

SUA

COUNTRY:
_____

CLUB:
_____

Answers: Italy – AC Milan, Spain – Real Madrid, England – Man Utd, USA – LA Galaxy.

Some of David Beckham's most memorable goals have come from set pieces. His trademark free kicks and penalties have earned his reputation as one of the game's all-time greats. These goals would never have gone in, though, without practice session after practice session.

1 Take a good run up, approaching the ball at an angle.

2 Keep your non-striking foot firmly on the ground, not too far away from the ball.

3 Wrapping your foot around the ball, connect with it off-centre, to create swerve in the air.

5 Leaning back slightly will help create extra height, if you need to get the ball up and over a defensive wall.

4 Swing through with your kicking foot, keeping your leg straight to get pace on the ball.

skills uncovered: SET PIECES

FREE KICKS

THE DAVID BECKHAM ACADEMY

1 — If you have to take a penalty kick, make up your mind where you want to put the ball and stick to it.

2 — The best places are the top corners, though the shot needs to be well-struck.

3 — If you shoot low and just inside either post, make sure you put enough pace on the ball.

4 — Blasting the ball straight down the middle is riskier. You have to be sure the 'keeper will dive either way.

5 — Everyone misses a penalty at some point. If you miss one, the chances are you'll score the next.

PENALTIES

MY MOVES

You've read about how to do each skill, now it's time to get active! Each time you practise these skills in the park, playground or garden, fill in the training chart to measure your progress.

TOP TIP!
Practise with both feet to keep defenders guessing when you're on the move in matches.

TEAM UP WITH FRIENDS OR FAMILY AND RATE THEIR SKILLS, TOO!

NO. OF TIMES PRACTISED

	1	2	3	4	5
WARM-UP AND WARM-DOWN					
BALL CONTROL					
PASSING					
DRIBBLING					
HEADING					
TACKLING					
TURNING					
VOLLEYING					
STRIKING					
SET PIECES					

NOW RATE YOUR OWN SKILLS ... WHICH MOVES HAVE YOU MASTERED? AND WHICH MOVES DO YOU NEED TO IMPROVE?

MY BEST SKILLS:

1 _____

2 _____

3 _____

SKILLS I NEED TO WORK ON:

1 _____

2 _____

3 _____

FOOTBALL GLOSSARY

ACADEMY	David Beckham's football school.
ASSIST	When a player helps a team-mate score.
ATTACK	The players that try to score a goal.
BOOTS	You'll need a pair of these to play the game on grass.
CAPTAIN	The team's leader, chosen by the manager.
COACH	Not the team bus, this is the person that trains players!
CLEAN SHEET	When the team doesn't let in a goal.
CORNER	A free kick taken from the corners of the pitch.
CROSS	To pass the ball across the field.
DEFENCE	The players that try to stop the opposition scoring a goal.
DRIBBLE	To move the ball along close to your feet.
FOUL	An action that is against the rules.
FREE KICK	When a foul is committed, the opposition is awarded a free kick.
FULL TIME	The end of the match, after 90 minutes in a pro game.
FORMATION	The way the team lines up, in defence, midfield and attack.
GOALKEEPER	An important player that tries to stop goals.
HALF TIME	The midway break in a match.
HAT-TRICK	Three goals scored by the same player in a single match.
HEADER	To hit the ball with your head.
JUGGLE	To keep the ball in the air using different parts of your body.
KICK-OFF	The start of a match.

KIT	Your shirt and shorts should fit comfortably and be kept clean.
MANAGER	The person in charge of the team, players and tactics.
MARK	To stay close to another player when defending the ball.
MIDFIELD	The middle of the pitch or group of players that play here.
NUTRITION	The study of food and diet.
OWN GOAL	When a player accidentally scores in the wrong goal.
PASS	To kick the ball to another player on the same team.
PENALTY	A free kick in the box, with one player against the 'keeper.
PITCH	The field of play.
RED CARD	Shown on its own or following a yellow card – the player must leave the pitch.
REFEREE	The person in charge of making sure a match is played fairly.
SHOOT	To kick the ball towards goal.
SPOT-KICK	Another name for a penalty kick.
SUBSTITUTE	A player that replaces another, through injury or for tactical reasons.
TACKLE	To try to take the ball from another player.
TACTICS	The manager's plans to win a match.
TEAM TALK	The manager's instructions to the team, usually before a match or at half time.
THROW-IN	A throw from the sidelines taken after the ball goes out of play.
VOLLEY	To kick the ball without it touching the ground.
WALL	A line of players defending a free kick.
WARM-DOWN	Make warming-down after matches part of your routine, just like when you …
WARM-UP	Start with jogging before you move on to your stretches.
WOODWORK	The frame of the goal – the crossbar and posts.
YELLOW CARD	Shown by the ref when a player makes a serious offence.

DAVID BECKHAM:
Legend

DAVID BECKHAM OBE

Clubs	Appearances	Goals
Manchester United	395	85
Real Madrid	158	20
LA Galaxy	30	5
AC Milan	12	2
England	110	17

HISTORY

Nationality **English**

Date of birth **2 May 1975**

Position **Midfield (Right, Central)**

TROPHIES

Premier League **1995-96, 1996-97, 1998-99, 1999-00, 2000-01, 2002-03**

FA Cup **1996, 1999**

UEFA Champions League **1999**

Intercontinental Cup **1999**

FA Youth Cup **1992**

La Liga **2006-07**

Spanish Super Cup **2003**

HONOURS

- England's most-capped outfield player of all time
- Only Englishman to have scored in three successive World Cups
- PFA Young Player of the Year 1997
- Winner of the treble (Premier League, FA Cup & UEFA Champions League) 1999 with Manchester Utd
- UEFA Champions League Footballer of the Year 1999
- Runner-up: European Footballer of the Year 1999; FIFA World Player of the Year 1999 and 2001
- BBC Sports Personality of the Year 2001

All information correct at time of going to print.

NEED HELP WITH YOUR FOOTBALL SKILLS?
WANT TO KNOW HOW TO GET IN SHAPE FOR YOUR NEXT MATCH?

THEN STEP INTO THE BOOTS OF A DAVID BECKHAM ACADEMY PLAYER WITH THESE GREAT STORY AND ACTIVITY BOOKS:

ISBN: 978 1 4052 4669 9   RRP: £4.99   ISBN: 978 1 4052 4670 5   RRP: £4.99

ISBN: 978 1 4052 4525 8   RRP: £4.99   ISBN: 978 1 4052 4524 1   RRP: £4.99

THESE AND MORE DAVID BECKHAM ACADEMY BOOKS ARE AVAILABLE NOW ON WWW.EGMONT.CO.UK OR IN ANY GOOD BOOKSHOP!

EGMONT

All David Beckham Academy titles unless otherwise stated: © 2009 Beckham Brand Limited. The David Beckham Academy words and logo are trademarks of Beckham Brand Limited. All rights reserved.

E0359